HIRE THE BEST
DITCH THE REST

A Simple
Team Building Strategy
For Exceptional Results

Richard S. George

Hire the Best – Ditch the Rest
THIRD EDITION

Published by
NOI Coach
A Division of Coach Services, Inc.
Waterford, MI

248-302-4444
noicoach.com

Dedication

When I released the 2nd edition, I never imaged I would one day be making the 3rd edition. As I did with the 2nd, I reaffirm my dedication to the two M's in my life:

My beautiful daughter Madeline, for giving me the motivation to keep moving forward.

And the other M (you know who you are), for giving me the greatest gift in the realization of how important "hiring the best" can be when it comes to finding a partner for the rest of your life.

While this is a business book, the lessons featured in this book extend well beyond boardrooms and cubic-les, as it can be used as a lesson for life itself, and I am happy to have been able to follow my own advice.

Also, a quick shout out to Chris Votey, who helped me take this book from the 2nd edition to the third.

TABLE OF CONTENTS

INTRODUCTION

WHY SHOULD YOU CARE WHAT I THINK?

If you're reading this, then it is fair to say that you are in a Leadership position. I will also presume you were elevated to that position as you are very good at what you do. Being a Leader requires a significant commitment to your employees. How you're defined as a Leader is reflected in how well your employees, your team, accomplishes the tasks necessary for the company.

So as the title states, "Why Should You Care What I Think?" That's a fair question. More than that, why should you spend your time, money, and effort reading what I've written. I will answer those question by telling you who I am, and why I know I am the right person for you to listen to, and this is a book you need to read.

I've spent over 25 years in the management and team building industry. I was hired into property management while still in college and found myself jumping leaps and bounds with one promotion after another. I moved from managing a few tasks to managing one site, to multiple sites, to entire companies. Starting with supervising just myself and eventually being a Leader to more than 500 employees.

Why was I so successful?

My success came because I surrounded myself with successful people. One of the first things a supervisor learns is that they can't do everything. There's too much to see, too much to do. Unfortunately, that's only the first part of the lesson, and it took a while before I learned the second part. You see, I delegated, but it included people I couldn't trust and couldn't rely on; these turned out to be valuable lessons (though costly).

My mother always told me that the school of hard knocks is the most expensive education out there. Delegating only works if you have the right team to delegate to. You must build a team that is right for the assets you're managing, for the people you're serving, and for each other. You need reshape the negative elements and remove toxic people, so the more ideal team members can be better.

Armed with those costly lessons, I continued my business success. In my last job, I became the director of a property management firm, with the goal of increasing the value of the portfolio by $10 million in 4 years. Not only did I meet that goal... my team increased the portfolio value by $22 million in 14 months.

Since I succeeded myself out of nearly three years of employment, I decided to share my experience and expertise with others. I started **NOI (Net Operating Income) Coach** in 2005, with the lion's share of my time spent meeting with companies and speaking to their managers about building strong teams.

As much as I come off sounding like, I don't know everything. Each of you reading this book knows something I don't – perhaps a lot more. I have been fortunate to have worked with enough terrific people, under the right circumstances, and put in the right amount of work, that I have something valuable to share.

Sometimes the pieces fell into place, but more often than not, I was dealt a hand, and I was required to make it work, required to mould my team into some-thing greater. On many occasions, I was awarded the privilege of creating my own team, and I proved my-self quite successful at picking the right people to get the job done.

That's why you should care what I think.

I'm not an attorney; I don't offer legal advice. What this book contains is commonly accepted management theory and best practices, based on research, experience, and some common sense. You should always refer to your company policies, procedures, and attorneys for any specific legal advice.

This is not a book of absolutes, nor is it the "Ten Commandments of Business". You'll choose what you get from this book, what you think will work for you while also ignoring those things that you don't think will work. As I do with all those I teach, I ask that you keep an open mind about what is featured in this book, as you will most definitely find a lot of what will work for you than what you think won't work for you.

If, however, you're looking for engaging business theory and complex case studies, you won't find them here. There are thousands of worthwhile books out there that will give you theory and case studies and involved explanations of every nuance of business. This book is designed for the business professional that recognizes the value of strong teams, knows their job, and wants some information they can put to use immediately.

This book is not really a "How-To", but more of a "Why-To". While there is useful information about how to do the more important tasks in teambuilding, such as how to identify toxic employees, how to hire the right people, and how to evaluate their performance, this book requires you to first accept the WHY. Why is anything featured in this book necessary for success at teambuilding? Without first accepting the WHY, you'll never be as successful as you hope to be with any projects you do.

It's a time-honored adage that if we do what we've always done, we'll get the results we've always gotten. This adage is so true when it comes to building teams, though it seems we continually fight with the same problems, just with different faces. It is time to do something different, and not only get a different result but to get an exceptional result.

Hire the Best – Ditch the Rest is designed to be used as soon as you finish the book. Heck, if you want to start using it before you finish the book, that's okay, too. The back of the book contains many of the important points in a set of easy-reference lists. You'll also find plenty of blank page space for taking notes, identifying those parts of the *Hire the Best – Ditch the Rest* process that you want to make work for you. That's right – go ahead, mark up the book. If the book just looks good on your shelf, it won't do you much good. If you want a clean copy, don't worry – we'll print more.

Your stories of trial and success are encouraged and welcome. This is a book that comes from people, and one thing that's the same about all people is this: They are all different!

Richard George
NOI Coach
June 2010
(Revised 2018)

Growth Is Good, But...

Most companies want to grow. Growth means more income, more income means more profits, and more profits mean more growth. Hypothetically, this cycle can continue endlessly. But growth for the sake of growth creates chaos. In your body, growth is good – it's how we mature – but uncontrolled growth is considered cancer. Companies who get too big too quickly end up in trouble. Teams that push forward without leadership, or without the right people involved, rush headlong towards failure.

In his book, "Good to Great", Jim Collins suggests that a business team is like people riding on the bus. When things aren't going well, stop the bus, make sure the right people are on the bus, and then let the team figure out where the bus is going and how to get there. Until you have the right people in place, your company cannot properly grow. Growth will occur, but not in a way that ensures success.

You might be hiring your team for the first time. You might inherit a team that already exists. You might be replacing team members to fill gaps in your existing group. Whatever the situation, you must have the right people in place to be successful. I realize this is not breaking news – we all know this if we've been in business longer than 15 minutes. What is surprising is how many good businesspeople know this, but don't act on that knowledge.

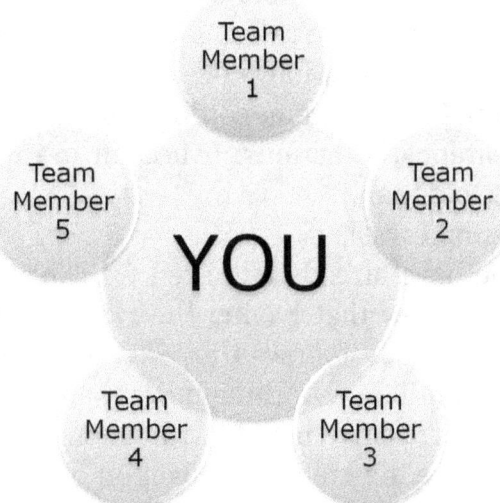

You Are Who You Know

Although we don't want to spend a lot of time on theory, there are some tried-and-true methods worth mentioning. Some are time-honored philosophies, while others are borne of my own experience and study.

The first of these is the idea that you are most influenced by those people closest to you. The best example of this is when we were children, as our sources of influence were our parents, our friends, our teachers, and our coaches. What we know of life was taught by these influences, as their presence in our lives helped developed who we became as teens well into adulthood.

Looking back, I remember once my father saying to me, "I don't like the kids you're hanging around with." At the time I didn't appreciate what he was saying – after all, what does it matter? I'm not them, so don't judge me by their attitudes, appearance, or actions. I thought to myself: "You're simply wrong, old man."

How wrong **I** was!

Since we have already admitted we can't do it all ourselves, and we know that having the right team in place is necessary, it naturally follows that we are, from a business and personal standpoint, nothing more than the sum total of those around us. The five people with whom we most closely associate will have the greatest impact on our thoughts, feelings, actions, our image, but most importantly how others categorize us.

We're All in This Together

Now, five isn't a magic number, just a typical, if not an arbitrary, number. It could be slightly more or fewer. I digress...

The point to focus on is that these are the people you rely on, the people you trust, the people who rely on and trust in you, the people whose opinions mean the most. Your personal and your business life depends on these few people, so it only makes sense that you want these to be the best possible people for your life – and for each other. They will determine your next success or failure.

NOTES

NOTES

HIRING
A TEAM

THE RIGHT TEAM

Did you know?

Most hiring decisions are wrong! According to multiple studies and accepted industry statistics, only about 25% of people hired for a job become high achievers. This doesn't mean the other 75% quit or are horrible, but only about one-quarter of the people who are hired "with great goals for the future" ever accomplish those goals.

If we assume that 25% of the hiring decisions are excellent, and another 25% are horrible, then half the decisions are, at best, so-so. A 25% success rate in baseball (a .250 batting average) will get you sent to the minors pretty quickly.

While you'll never be 100% - life just isn't that predictable – you can improve your batting average. Imagine, if you could hire that exceptional person two times out of four instead of just one out of four. More than that, you could eliminate hiring that lousy person altogether, hiring two other so-so workers. You'd be thrilled, and your success would skyrocket.

Whether we're hiring a team from scratch or replacing someone in an already existing group, there are four primary truths in hiring. I know I make it sound easy, and in fact, the process is rather simplistic, but it is still a challenge to accomplish. In the next part, we will explore those four truths, so when it comes time to hire that team member, you'll have more tools at your disposal.

The Four Hiring Truths

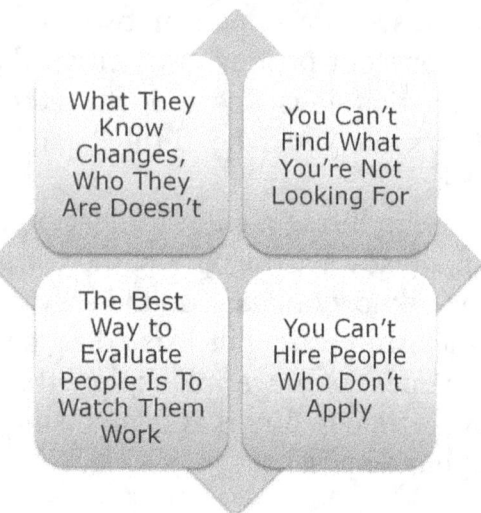

You Can't Find What You're Not Looking For

The best way to select people who will thrive in your company is to identify the personal characteristics of those who already thrive. Look at your people. What is it about Reggie that makes him successful? Why is Helen enthused about coming to work? When Martin gets that gleam in his eye because he has solved a problem, where does that come from? Work to understand your star performers' attributes, and then look for others who share those qualities.

Find the Target First
Then Shoot the Arrow

Even the best archer in the world cannot succeed unless they know the target. If you take away the net in hockey, no one can score. Likewise, you wouldn't start painting a room without first knowing what color you wanted the walls to be. You wouldn't start driving to an important meeting without first understanding where that meeting was supposed to take place.

The hiring process is no different. If you start recruiting, interviewing, and sorting through candidates without first knowing:

- What you're hiring for
- The qualities you need
- The personalities that will fit in your team
- The attitudes you want

...then you're an archer who is flinging arrows through the air, hoping one will land on the target – but even then, never knowing if you hit the target because you don't know what the target is.

It is a mistake to hire someone with a blurry picture. Most of us do this by simply utilizing the job description as our guide to determine whether a candidate qualifies, which assumes the job description is accurate to begin with.

Even if you have a clear understanding of what the job is, using the job description as a sole metric, only addresses their skills, experience, and knowledge. It does not paint a clear picture of who they are, from their behavioral characteristics to their general attitude about their potential job (or in life).

Honestly, if that is all you use to hire someone, then there is practically no reason to interview someone, and you can save a lot of time by looking at resumes and deciding based on how good they look on paper.

If you want to *Hire The Best - Ditch The Rest*, then you must have a crystal clear, 4K Ultra HD, 3-D image of the type of person you want to hire. Take a close and critical look at where you have been and where you are, starting with: **why you're hiring in the first place.**

Then look with, the same closeness and critical eye, at where you want this person to be – what do you want to be different from the person you are replacing (or what do you want to add to your team). You must also be willing to spend the time it will take to find that person, because – as will be repeated many times in this book – URGENCY is fatal to hiring success.

Only when you have a clear target in sight and know the best way to reach the bullseye, you can release the arrow. Until you have that clear picture and are willing and able to invest the time, you have no business recruiting and interviewing, and certainly no business hiring.

Hiring Is Like
Trying to Find A Mate

The hiring process mentioned earlier, that uses just job descriptions to determine whether someone should be hired or not, is more like online dating than say a blind date a friend sets up. Even those who have never tried online dating are familiar enough with how it works: you start by posting a profile on a dating site, not unlike submitting a resume to an employer; detailing what you do, what you like and dislike, and maybe even what you're looking for in a relationship.

You, of course, want to put your best foot forward, only revealing what makes you look like the best match, and keep hidden what may be less desirable, until someone gets to know you. It seems quite manipulative that people do this, whether for online dating or applying for a job, but it's normal human behavior.

Using myself as an example, I might put on an online dating profile: I love taking long walks on the beach, deep philosophical conversations until the wee hours of the morning, and skydiving. My ex-wife, however, would add many unflattering things to that: I leave dirty socks under the coffee table, I refuse to put the toilet seat down, and other perhaps a few other things.

If you're looking at online dating sites because you're thinking about a relationship, the first thing you'll do is read that profile. Okay, maybe the first thing you do is look at the picture, but that's part of the screening process people use in "hiring" a mate – they look for a particular type. How someone presents themselves (visually) can say a lot about who they are.

Once you inspect them visually, you'll evaluate their words:

- Is this the kind of person I would enjoy meeting?
- Do I think this is an accurate description?
- Do they smoke?
- How often do they drink?
- Nude bungee jumping!?

You'll probably even "Google" that person to see if there's any information floating across the Web that would be useful in your evaluation, or reverse image search to see if they stole their photo from another website, not unlike calling references or previous employers. You'll likely do all this before ever talking to this person.

Up to this point, everything looks good. This may be someone you'd enjoy spending time with. However, you'll know that not everyone is candid with their profiles, as you yourself may not have been. Thus, it's time to establish communication.

Chatting online can be seen as a "pre-screening interview", like an employer emailing someone to get basic information beyond their resume, or even doing a phone interview. You ask some more direct questions and see how they respond in reference to what they put on their profile and/or resume. Is it consistent, or do they act differently than they presented themselves?

Of course, of course, nothing beats a face-to-face meeting. A pre-screening can only tell you so much, and in many ways suffers the same problems as posting an online profile. There is a certain level of anonymity people feel when there is a lack of face-to-face, which is why to truly know a person, you must meet with them.

Wouldn't it be great if this online dating site you are using had buttons that said:

How much easier dating would be?! Well, in the business world we have these buttons available to us. Unfortunately, because of urgency to hire, lack of knowledge, or because of a lack of courage to make the effort, we don't use them.

Most of us wouldn't dream of entering into a relationship without knowing a lot about the person we're dealing with, but for many people the hiring process is quick, sloppy, and based on something we like to call "a gut feeling." More often than not we find our gut feeling was wrong, but when it's time to replace that lousy employee – after a long, tedious, time-consuming, life-altering, messy break-up – we go back to that tried but untrue method.

Why?

- You might think it's because you don't have the time.
- You might think it's because you don't have the resources.
- You might think that it's because your gut feeling is so much better.

You'd be wrong in every case.

During the recruiting and hiring process, we have many tools that go unused. In addition to everything avail-able in the dating scenario – resumes, multiple contact options, In-ternet research – we have these other tools we just ment-ioned: criminal background checks, credit reports, and, most importantly, their past employers.

Unlike the dating world, you can easily contact ex-re-lationships and find out how that person behaved, what they accomplished, and how they interacted with others. We have that opportunity, but all too often it is thrown away.

In one of my favorite TV shows, there is a detective that tries to make a fellow officer understand that what things appear to be and what they are can be very different. He sums it up beautifully when he says, "Everything is a sit-uation."

When you decide to check credit reports, criminal back-grounds, and references, you recognize that you're not look-ing at any one factor in a vacuum.

Checking the credit report and finding it excellent might tell you the person practices personal responsibility. The problem with credit reports is that it doesn't reveal be-yond the most basic information and you may desire to ex-plore the results further as it relates to your expectations.

Maybe the person doesn't practice personal responsibility; maybe – like a very good friend of mine – his house burned down (taking the car with it), and his wife demanded a di-vorce, all within a few days' time. For a period of time, he says, his credit report was less-than-stellar.

A criminal background could indicate a misspent youth, or it could indicate a problem. A bad reference check could mean he has trouble relating to others, or it could mean their boss had that difficulty. You will have to evaluate the information, but you cannot evaluate the information un-less you have it in front of you.

Everything is a situation.

Look Beyond The Resume
(Hire For Attitude – Train For Skill)

The resume will show the prospective employee at their best – at least, it should. It will often claim intelligence and experience and accomplishment. These are fantastic, but when hiring for a team, you need more.

The ultimate employee is someone whose devotion to customer and company is a personal mission, a sense that the "cause" comes before their own needs. Will this person look beyond the job description to work within a team as a full-fledged invested member?

What we're looking for in a team member is someone with an attitude, a genuineness, a commitment to what it takes to be one of us. This doesn't mean you want to hire people solely for their attitude and enthusiasm, any more than you'd marry someone just because of their looks.

The truth of the matter is, you're not picking someone just for you; you're choosing for the team, so you want someone with the skills to do the job, but someone who'll fit in well with the team. Not everyone with a car and a driver's license would be great as at pizza delivery, nor would those who are a chatterbox would be good at public speaking.

The most important information you can get from an interview is what that candidate wants. If they give you a clear image of their goals, their wants and their desires from a job, you have a better chance of getting performance to match that image. If the picture is fuzzy and vague, fuzzy and vague could be the performance you'll see.

Look For Those Willing
To "Join Your Cult"

They are sometimes hard to find – rare, even. You'll almost certainly have some success finding the candidate who looks beyond the job description, who has a true customer-and-team attitude. But can you find someone willing to really join your cult, who can adopt the passion and sense of excitement you bring to your work? Can you find someone fanatical? Can you find someone just a little bit insane?

On television and in the movies, it's those characters who are just a little bit nuts about what they do that makes them both interesting and successful. No one cares that much about Bruce Wayne... but Batman is a hero fighting crime, getting things done, kicking some butt. Of course, he's dressed as a giant bat, which is a little bit nuts – but so what?

When you can identify those cult-joiners, the people willing to buy into your team mission with more than just passion – with obsession – you have a gem.

Of course, this only works if you have that passion... that obsession. If you don't, it's unlikely you'll recognize it in others, and it's equally unlikely that they can sustain it long if you're not reinforcing it.

So – be that nut!

Why Not Just Hire Myself?

Early in your career you realized that you were successful. You went through a quick thought process:

"I've been promoted, often."
"I must be good."
"I should hire people just like me!"

Logical? Sure, if you're hiring people for the same position spread across the country, doing the same job you are, in the same way.

You have a unique, and likely excellent, set of skills and experience. Your people see you as a leader; maybe you see yourself as a leader, and you want to re-create for your team what brought you to this point in your success.

You don't, however, know everything, and you have your own set of human limitations. You're not looking for more of you, because that means that you have a team full of people who only know what you know, only see things how you see them, and have the same limitations that you have. You haven't filled the gaps in your team in this case, you've widened them.

If you hire people just like you, you've engaged in a sort of corporate inbreeding that dilutes the informational and creative gene pool. To attempt to try to find our own "mini-me" is a mistake when hiring. We need people with behavioral patterns, skills sets, and characteristics that complement and enhance ourselves and our team.

The Popeye Factor

"I Yam what I Yam."

The most common and fatal mistake in hiring is finding someone with the wrong mindset and hiring them with the vow *"We can change 'em."* You can't. **What they know changes; who they are doesn't**. Popeye was right when he said, *"I yam what I yam."*

Does this ring true to you when you think about your own dating life, as we mentioned before? When you started dating So-And-So (who comes from a long and distinguished line of So-And-Sos), did you say to yourself, "I like this person a lot. With time I am sure I can change the things I don't like." Of course, that didn't happen. Either we became used to them and accepted those things we didn't like, or we broke up with them.

In business, we end up adapting our business to the people around us; the people don't change for our sakes. We're not talking skills here, but character and personality. We're not looking for clones, and we're not expecting people to be exactly how we want them to be – both are impossible. We just need to remember that people don't change – how we value or devalue them, does.

Who Knew?
(Hint: You Should Have.)

Chances are good that somewhere in the past you have made a bad hiring decision. Someone you hired didn't work out – or worse, caused havoc among your team. You probably thought to yourself, "Wow, I never saw that coming!" Well, chances are, unless you utilized all your resources and hired in a slow, methodical, and complete process, you should have.

No hiring process is perfect. Sometimes the information isn't there, and it's impossible to tell that someone will not work out well. There are no hard statistics on this, but if you didn't do reference checks, if you didn't check all those aspects of a candidate's past that are truly important to your team and its success, and if you didn't address any concerns you have before hiring, then to later throw your arms up and say, "Who knew...?" denies the fact that you should have known.

No candidate is going to tell you during the interview that they will be a horrible team member, they will try to do the least possible amount of work, and that their results will disappoint.

Or will they?

Learning is about listening. If you practice the 80-20 Rule for interviews, you have a much better chance of learning about your applicant, and you're giving them a chance to tell you almost everything you need to know about their attitude, their goals, and their true approach to the workday.

The 80-20 Rule:
Listen 80% of the time;
talk no more than 20% of the time.

One of the first pieces of advice hiring coaches give to potential applicants is to get the interviewer talking. We love the sound of our own voice, and we're happy about our accomplishments. If we spend the interview talking instead of listening, when it is over we'll come away feeling good. We won't know much about the candidate, but we'll have that "gut feeling" about them because they really made us feel good. We don't realize that we felt good because we spent the whole time talking about ourselves!

One great way to prevent talking too much is to prepare an interview guide. When you sit down to talk you will want to have your questions already prepared. You know the kind of person you want, so you know the questions you want to ask. If you've already checked references and other information, then you'll definitely have follow-up questions.

The value of the interview guide, above and beyond making sure you get the right information, is that it will help keep you from talking too much. It will also help you get rid of the fear of silence.

When you ask a particularly good question, one which requires thought on the part of the candidate, it's okay to sit in silence. It's a compliment to your question and a boon to the applicant. Too often we get uncomfortable and try to fill the silence by answering the questions ourselves, or we move on and never learn the answer that we seek. The phrase, "Just take your time and think about it" will reap benefits for both of you.

Question and listen.

Resources

You can find hundreds of useful books which will detail the hiring process and give you step-by-step instructions. Find them, use them. Some traditional worthwhile methods and resources include:

Interview Guides – Is conducting that interview not your strong suit? You can find guides that will take you through the process question-by-question, not only helping you find the right person but keeping you out of legal hot water. As already mentioned, it will also help you to listen, which is where learning is born.

Make sure that your questions are not simple yes/no type questions. Using behavior-based questions enables us to find out what people are likely to do based on what they have done.

Skills-Based Testing – It is okay to verify that people have the necessary skills needed to perform a job. I think there'd be nothing worse than to hire your new payroll clerk, only to discover they cannot multiply.

The 80/20 Rule – NOTHING works better than listening

References – As already mentioned, these are critical. What people will do is best shown by what they have done in the past.

In our litigious-crazy world, many companies nowadays have "gag policies" that prohibit them from giving us any information during a reference check, or they can simply offer the equivalent of name, rank and serial number. That's unfortunate; when you find someone willing to provide unbiased and complete information, it's a real treat.

Don't think that you can't learn something from even the most basic information, however. When you call, listen for the lilt and the tone in the voice of the person you're talking to, if they recognize the person you're calling about. Do they sound happy to hear that name, or did it sound like you'd just insulted someone's mother?

Even if you don't get the tone, can't determine whether this person was liked, or whether they would be shot on sight when entering the building, at the very least you can verify the information on the application. With that, you've done more due diligence than half the people hiring out there.

Recruiting Agencies – Whether you use a third-party agency to recruit applicants or not isn't the big issue. They are available, and most are excellent, but the critical point is that you cannot hire people who don't apply. Your recruiting should be active; you should be seeking people with the skills you want, not waiting for them to randomly drop by or magically know your needs.

Start your recruiting close to home, and always treat it as seriously as any other work process – even more so because you're betting your future on the people you hire.

Recruiting agencies have access to people that are already employed but are discreetly looking to join a team that fits their personal mission statement better. Over the last decade or so new methods have come into use, and they give you new ways to observe and learn about your potential team member.

On-The-Job Interviewing – Many companies use a one to three days on-the-job paid interview to assess possible team members. This process allows the candidate to explore what the job entails, and for the employer to observe some of the skills that were alluded to in the resume. Interaction with the rest of the team can highlight strengths of the new person or identify possible issues.

Having gone through some on-the-job interviews myself I endorse them enthusiastically. I once declined a job because after the day-long on-the-job interview I knew I wasn't the right fit for that team (specifically, the culture of that team), and I suspect they knew it, too.

There's probably no "typical" day in your world, but you can simulate many of the events your candidate will encounter and see how they react. If people really want to work for you, they will invest the time and effort. You really can't afford to make a bad decision.

The on-the-job interview is not always possible. If someone already has a job and would have to give notice, working for you would not make sense. But where possible, where legal, where logical, **the best way to evaluate someone is to watch them work!**

Hire the Best – Ditch the Rest – It's illegal to profile based on race, religion, sex, etc., but it is perfectly okay to profile based on behavior. Many respected companies offer behavioral surveys which can help you identify styles among your candidates; from this, you can determine what style would be a better fit with your team.

Some of the areas where you can test for patterns and approaches include:

- Behavioral
- Personality
- Skills
- Leadership
- Responsibility
- Honesty
- Reliability

Remember – The truest test of how someone will perform in the future is how they have performed in the past.

Group Interviewing – As mentioned before, you're not just hiring for you; you're hiring for the whole team. So, let the team interview. Let the candidate ask questions of the team, and let the team get to know the applicant. Jane will ask questions Ronald didn't think of, and Sam will notice some signals that Sally missed.

Unique Interview Locales – The interview doesn't have to take place in your office. There may be a need for privacy during some parts of the conversation, but spending the time walking through the offices or the store, where you can point out people and functions, ask questions, and answer them, can make the interview more informative.

Being able to move around will often make your applicant more relaxed – not worried so much about fidgeting – and relaxed people talk more, tell you more about themselves, open up in a more complete manner. Interviewing isn't always a walk in the park, but that doesn't mean it can't include a walk in the park.

Recruiting Through Social Networking Sites – There have been plenty of stories in the news about employees and potential employees having their careers damaged through unfortunate choices posted on social networking sites. Much less has been written about how social networking on the Internet (Facebook, Twitter, LinkedIn, plus hundreds of other closed or specialized sites, such as Forums or Reddit) is being used to find and recruit strong team members.

Over the last few years, social networking sites on the Web have followed only personal referrals as the most valued source for finding good employment candidates. It is valued far more than any of the thousands of Internet job boards, newspaper ads, or job fairs. Partly because of its economic factor, but mostly because it promotes open and free communication long before any formal interview process takes place, social networking is becoming the #1 recruiting method in America.

Urgency – The Killer of
Hiring Successfully

Your need to hire may have come suddenly, as has been mentioned before, but urgency – the need to do it right now – is the silver bullet that can kill your process for hiring a successful person. Like a broken record (for those of you who remember what vinyl sounds like), I will repeat this phrase again and again: Take your time. You may not feel you have the time, but you certainly don't have the time, or the money, to make the wrong decision on who you hire.

Rewarding employment is an investment in the person you hired, and in making the wrong decision may require future hiring's as a replacement, which can be costly. Most people hire too quickly and then, in turn, take too long to fire, which is utterly backwards. Take your time hiring, and do less firing.

A warm body is NOT better than nobody - "nobody" doesn't draw a paycheck; "nobody" can't poison your team's chemistry; "nobody" won't undermine your goals.

The Four Hiring Truths, again:

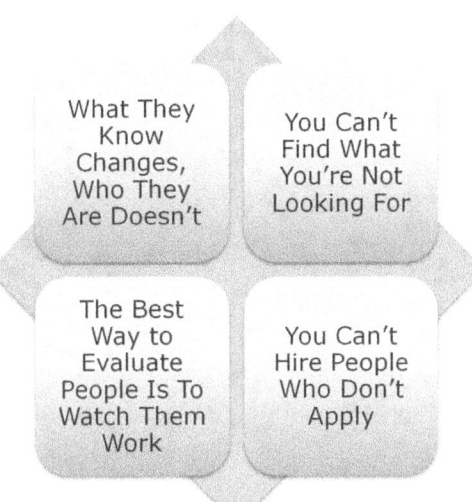

Hiring is a skill, and it is an art. There are people for whom it comes naturally and others who must learn it – but the fact is, everyone can learn it, and anyone who wants to build a reliable and successful team needs to learn it.

The overarching idea is that you hire hard, then manage easy. If you don't – if hiring is too easy, then you probably will have to manage hard!

NOTES

NOTES

COURAGE FACTOR
OF LEADERSHIP

COURAGE & LEADERSHIP

Many years ago, I was complaining to my then wife about some of the employee issues that I was having at the office (specifically, Jim --- ARRRGGH). She said something that has impacted the rest of my life. I think she said this just to shut up my complaining, but she asked me, "What if Jim gave you his two-week notice tomorrow morning, how would you feel?" I had to think about this for a while, but ultimately the answer was that I would be relieved. She said then, "I think you have your answer. What are you going to do about it?"

I pondered this for a while and ultimately decided to terminate Jim. This question became what I call The Question. So, I took this concept a few steps further: I decided to ask myself this question quarterly of all my employees. There are three possible answers for each employee:

44

Level One: I would be devastated
Level Two: Well, it wouldn't be the end of the world - I guess it's time to start recruiting
Level Three: I would be relieved

For every employee that I felt the first way about, it meant that I needed to appreciate them more, whether it be with signs of appreciation or compensation.

For every employee that I felt the second way about, it meant that I needed to engage in some sort of coaching and mentoring to bring them up to the level of number one.

For every employee that I would be relieved if they gave notice, I needed to take decisive action, whether that meant terminating the employment or try to fix the issues that caused me to feel this way.

I started using this tactic religiously for about two years with amazing results when it came to building teams, but the flaw that I learned was that this was an entirely internal process. I would think about this question, and then answer it to myself, but selfishly I would keep the answers to myself. I would then - subversively - try to manipulate my teammates into moving into Level One (devastation if they quit) by quietly trying to correct the behaviors or attitudes that made me feel otherwise.

Rules For Asking The Question....

- **The Question** should never be asked when you're mad at your employee. It's not something to be tainted by emotions. It's a regular, but not daily, evaluation of that person's overall value to the team.

- **The Question** should be based on skills, attitude, and effect on the rest of the team, not your opinion of their style or personal beliefs. It's not an excuse for getting rid of someone you don't agree with.

- Each answer to **The Question** demands some type of action. If you would be devastated, take steps to make sure it doesn't happen. If you would be indifferent, find out why and work to make that person able to devastate you. If you would be relieved, you must choose either to fire or fix the issues.

- Finally, as I will now explain, **DON'T KEEP IT A SECRET!**

One day I was thinking about something I learned early in my budding career, and that is the power of **Courageous Conversation**. It made me think, "Why am I keeping this to myself?" So, I started sharing my answers with the respective employees. This took the good results that I was already getting and made them exceptional.

Finally, I had found the formula for building exponentially better teams, while building relationships with my teammates that have proven the strength to last a lifetime. It was no surprise that my employees/teammates were craving the direct, compassionate, and courageous conversations to build themselves to be the strong Leaders that many of them have become.

Through trial and error, I was able to identify some of the key components of having a courageous conversation like this, and it helped me to overcome the fear that is associated with difficult communications. I identified seven steps to having a courageous conversation, which is featured down below.

REMEMBER: if you are still at the place of "blaming or judging", you need to get over that first before moving forward. The overruling message for success is to do it with your heart, soul, and compassion.

Seven Steps to Having That Courageous Conversation

1. Choose the person that you don't feel 100% about.
2. Identify clearly the truth/core of what you want to express.
3. Identify the worst possible outcome you can imagine.
4. Accept that possibility. Now, let it go.
5. Remember that it's OK to feel uncomfortable, even terrified. In fact, you probably should feel uncomfortable; that will add the compassion piece to your message. The greater the fear, the more you have to gain.

6. Embrace the moment; this is the equivalent to crowning the first giant hill of a rollercoaster. You are now committed to a prosperous future.
7. Go For It! Accept what you get as the best possible outcome.

This is definitely not the coward's method. You must be committed to a dramatically improved future for the employee as well as yourself, and there should be no doubt in the mind of your employee about this conviction.

Above all, be compassionate. A lot of leaders take pride in the fact that they are "direct", that they tell it like it is, that they don't mince words. I am not saying to sugar coat it, just be certain that you are strategic with your communication. Don't let your words be bullets, because then you have a wounded employee, and a wounded employee will focus more in how they are hurt than the task they must accomplish. You need an employee that comes out with full strength to meet the challenges that lay ahead of them.

The simple way to look at it is this: If someone isn't doing the job, either they aren't good enough (which means they should be terminated), they aren't a good fit for the team (in which case letting them go is a favor), or they were not given the tools or training to do the job. The courageous leader decides which of these is true, and acts on it.

Where Is Your Loyalty?

As you look at your employees and decide their value to the team, and to your company (and, by extension, to you), it's worthwhile to think about where your loyalties lie. Unquestionably, if this person is a member of your team, you feel some sense of loyalty to them, regardless of how you answered The Question. Probably, though, you realize your loyalty is to the team as a whole, more so than any individual.

That's only partly true.

Most of us are middle managers, which means we lead one team, but that we're also part of another team lead by someone else. Where is your loyalty? You might think that you're like the captain of a ship, and decide that you must think of your crew first – after all, they count on you, trust you, rely on your, and need you to guide them. Noble thoughts, but misguided.

Just as the Captain of a ship might be told to take their ship and crew on a dangerous mission, your team, as a whole, must serve the larger team. Just as you think of each member of your team as a part of the whole, your team itself is considered one part of a much larger whole, so in the end, you serve the whole, by leading your team effectively.

When you assemble your team, if you've done it right, they are people who are not necessarily friends (they could be), but people who have trust in group accountability. They understand that the team matters, but the team as part of the whole matters more.

NOTES

NOTES

THE
TWELVE EMPLOYEES

THE TWELVE EMPLOYEES

No employee is perfect. No one is always on time, gives complete attention and focus to every project in every situation, is able to work with everyone else, never complains, and makes the best coffee on the planet. We all have our strengths and weaknesses and quirks. That's not to say we don't have people who think they are perfect – probably we've all thought that at some point – but they, and we, are not.

Most of the twelve types we describe here are in terms of what makes them difficult. Not all employees are difficult, and those who are might still be valuable members of your team. Making them better members of your team (or deciding they shouldn't be) starts with identifying the issues.

As you progress through these 12 types of employees, I challenge you to think about your teams, both past and present, to see if you have or have had any of these. My next challenge is for you to think about your career and see if you have ever – or correctly do – fit into any of these categories.

#1
The "Not-So Go-Getter"

It's the end of a long week. Your team has worked hard, accomplished a lot, and you're confident about the results that will come. As you head out the door on Friday evening, you see Andy, one of the members of your team. It occurs to you that you haven't talked to Andy all week.

He's been at the meetings but hasn't had anything to say, and you never stopped by his office. As you pass in the hall, you stop and say hello, and goodbye for the weekend. Curiosity grabs you, and you ask, "So, Andy, we never had a chance to talk this week. What did you accomplish?" Andy's face goes slightly white – and you've seen that stare before: Last fall when you were driving along the country road and almost hit a deer that was the blank look on the face of the deer staring at your headlights.

Andy is a nice guy. Andy does decent work when you give him an assignment. If you ask for it in three days, you'll have it in three days (but never two). If you ask for an opinion, he'll provide it, but only if you ask. He'll never stop by your office. He has good ideas when you can pull them out.

Andy is a nice guy – but Andy is a Not-So-Go-Getter. You can spot Andy because he:
- Just moves along through the day
- Does what they're told – no more and no less
- Has no natural initiative instincts

Since Andy does a good job when you give him assignments and deadlines, he can be a worthwhile member of your team, as long as you make sure he has assignments and deadlines with specific instructions. Andy isn't going to lead your team, because that would mean he'd have to focus on more than the minimum. He's a good follower – but he has to be led all the time, which can create problems.

Sometimes the Not-So-Go-Getter is a product of the old style of management which said, "I don't pay you to think." This person might have had initiative at some point, but it was stripped away by indifference or criticism. If you think you can find that Go-Getter trapped inside, go for it.

Write Out a List of Employees
You Have That Fit This Description

#2
The "Complainer"

The results are in: Success! Your team exceeded its goals, and you've just shared the good news with everyone. After handshakes and pats on the back and the knowledge that rewards are just around the corner, you head back to your office.

As you pass Barry's door you hear him talking with another team member. You don't stop (you've learned from past experience not to do that too often), but you slow down long enough to hear him say:

> *"Sure, but that just means they'll expect more from us every time. And do you think we'll get a raise for our hard work? I bet we won't. And if we do it won't be much, I can guarantee you that. Besides, they'll just use that to make us work longer hours. And for another thing..."*

You realize that slowing down was a bad idea. Barry is a complainer, and you can spot him because he:
- Whines about everything
- Complains whether it is bad or good
- Tells others that all good things have ulterior motives

Barry is probably smart and contributes to your success, but since he never sees anything positively, he never feels that success. Thus, he works hard to make others feel as down as he does.

It's likely that the other team members have become used to Barry, and roll their eyes toward each other when they listen to his diatribes. The Complainer can be a minor annoyance, but can also be very disruptive.

Write Out a List of Employees
You Have That Fit This Description

#3
The "Paycheck Gatherer"

You always wondered why Cassie's parents didn't just name her Cash – because it seems that's the only thing she wants to talk about. You can almost see the tension in the air every other week as Friday approaches and Cassie starts to sweat, waiting for the payroll to arrive.

It's as if she thinks this will be the week she doesn't get paid, that suddenly the company has decided not to pay for the work. It's with a gasp of relief she grabs her envelope and opens it frantically. She's never satisfied, even though it's the same amount she got the last payday.

Of course, that's not as bad as last week, when Cassie came into your office to tell you that she just bought a new car – so she needs a raise to pay for it!

Cassie is a paycheck gatherer, and you identify her by:

- Always concerned about payroll: When is it coming? Will it be late? How about a raise?
- When they spend money, it's your responsibility to cover the cost.
- Many conversations center around what they're "entitled" to".

Where people like Cassie become a problem isn't usually in their work performance. What she's complaining about has little to do with work, so it would be easy to dismiss it as a minor annoyance. When she is vocal, though, she creates a wave of negative energy that covers your office. She takes the focus away from the team and constantly tries to place it on herself, what she should be worth (in her mind) and what she needs.

Write Out a List of Employees
You Have That Fit This Description

#4
The "Anti-Change Agent"

When you hired Darrel, you were excited, and for a long time, you felt justified in bringing him on the team. He learned the job quickly and did it with energy and a great spirit of cooperation.

Unfortunately, you didn't see the other side of Darrel until last fall when you had to make changes in the work process. Darrel didn't just like the way things worked before; he was in love with it. In fact, Darrel hates change – any kind of change. If you change the decision process, it's as though you were asking him to learn binary code.

Darrel is the Anti-Change Agent, one of those who:
- Fights every change in the team or the organization, no matter how slight.
- Policies, procedures, job descriptions, and even the color of the walls were all better "the way we used to do it."

Darrel frustrates everyone, which is damaging to the team. You know that if he would just open his mind to the idea that change can be good and should be given a chance, he'd learn that for himself, but he is unwilling. More than just an annoyance, when he succeeds in convincing others that change is bad, he is destructive.

Anti-Change agents are often created from fear. Fear of failure and fear of looking silly will stop many people from accepting change. Sometimes all it takes is showing that person that failure is okay and that we all look silly from time to time.

Write Out a List of Employees
You Have That Fit This Description

#5
The "Overwhelmed" Employee

Nobody works harder than Ellen. You know this because Ellen always tells you so. Day in and day out, no one looks more worried, moves about more frantically, talks about deadlines and how busy she is, than Ellen.

Her work output is average at best, and for a long time you weren't entirely sure what was filling up her day, but then it hits you: Ellen fills her day with thinking about how full her day is. Ellen is so befuddled you saw her to-do list for today and weren't surprised to see it included "Write tomorrow's to-do list."

Ellen is the Overwhelmed Employee. You can identify her type by the fact:

- She can never find enough time in the day to create more chaos.
- She spends more time worrying and talking about what she has to do than actually doing what she has to do.

If you could get Ellen's work output to approach her perception of her workload, then you know you'd really have something! Right now, you'd be happy if you just didn't have to hear about it.

Write Out a List of Employees
You Have That Fit This Description

#6
The "That's Not My Job" Employee

Frank has his job description memorized. He can tell you what he's supposed to do, and what he's not supposed to do – to which he does, daily and with vigor. There's just one part of his job description that he treats as if it were a foreign tongue: the part where it says, "Other tasks as assigned." Frank was hired to do a specific job, and anything else is an effrontery to his intelligence, his honor, and his sense of fair play.

Frank is the "That's Not My Job" employee. This kind of employees follows these philosophies:

- Their job description should be taken literally, but only using their own literal definition.
- They think life should be fair and everything should run as they expect it to run.
- They have no understanding of the team concept.

Frank's self-centered nature is damaging to the team. In the sports world, he's the athlete with a multi-million-dollar contract who doesn't show up for training camp, thinking of his pride and his "value" over the needs of the team. It can be contagious. At its mildest, Frank creates more work for others, especially those who are willing to make sacrifices for the team. At his worst, he can be a cancer.

Write Out a List of Employees You Have That Fit This Description

#7
The "Socialite" Employee

There's not much you can say about Gabby that hasn't already been said before... mostly by Gabby. You think to yourself: "Did her parents change her name to Gabby after she learned to talk?" The eight-hour workday, according to her internal calendar, has a 4½ hour built-in segment for talking – that's not counting lunch. Gabby knows what everyone is up to, even if she has to make some of it up along the way. After all, it could be true for all she knows.

Gabby is friendly, outgoing, and outside the workplace probably fun to be around. In the workplace though, she's a giant vacuum, sucking the time and energy out of everyone's workday.

This is the Socialite employee, who easily standout by their presence, by:

- Distracting the attention of others by constantly talking.
- Being the source of the latest rumors.
- Ignoring facts, as they are not important; those can be made up along the way.

Gabby seems to get away with being the Socialite for a long time simply because she is very likeable. The damage to the team is only recognized slowly, but that damage can be severe.

Write Out a List of Employees
You Have That Fit This Description

#8
The "Clock Watcher"

Harriet arrives for work on time every day, at 7:59. Sometimes you think she has spent hours timing the traffic, the parking, and the elevator as some sort of personal experiment to see how close to 8:00 am she can arrive. In reality, Harriet is just so worried that she might actually do some work that's not on the clock, she'll go to great length to prevent it.

Harriet won't be late, especially when it comes to the end of the day. Don't even think of starting a conversation with her at 4:45 pm, because she's already got her desk cleared, coat at the ready, and her car keys in his hand.

While she is there, she does a fine job, but Harriet is a Clockwatcher, and they are recognizable because:

- They always know precisely the number of minutes from this moment in time to 5:00 pm.
- They are much like the Paycheck Gatherer in that their main concern is pay, and not their accomplishments or the team.

Harriet is easy to spot, but difficult to find fault with, initially. She can easily justify that she puts in her time, and always has a reason why she can't stay late or come early - which may, in fact, be justifiable.

However, it's the constant nature of her attitude and the way it affects others in the long haul that makes Harriet and other Clockwatchers difficult, and possibly damaging.

Write Out a List of Employees You Have That Fit This Description

#9
The "Nosey" Employee

"Why do you do that?"
"What's this for?"
"How come you said this to him?"
"I think I just saw him go into Frank's office."
"Well, she makes $3,000 a year more than
you, so let her do it."
"Aren't you supposed to be at that sales
meeting in ten minutes?"

Irvine knows it all; that is, he knows it all about every-one else. You considered that maybe he works for the CIA and has everyone's office bugged, that's how much he seems to know. He knows everything except that he's not getting the job done.

Irvine is a Nosey employee, and they're hard to miss:
- Always seems to know all the dirt.
- Mysteriously knows what everyone makes in salary.
- Seems to know where you are (or should be) at all times.
- Never seems to know they're failing.

Unlike the Socialite, who wants to be everyone's friend, the Nosey employee wants to be everyone's newsagent. The team doesn't need a newsagent, and most of the news is either superfluous or damaging. The Nosey Employee is sel-dom just an annoyance.

81

Write Out a List of Employees
You Have That Fit This Description

#10
The "I Deserve Your Job" Employee

When you hired Joanne, she was very adamant that her goal was to take over your job one day. You liked that; it showed drive and ambition. What you didn't expect was that Joanne expected you to step down right away. Almost from the minute she arrived, Joanne let it be known that she knew more than you and the others. She even knows more than the guy who's worked there since 1996.

The "I Deserve Your Job" employee doesn't just have an ego – they keep a spare in their desk drawer and one in the glove compartment of their car. The "I Deserve You Job Employee" can be easily identified:

- Was hired into an entry-level position and cannot understand why they aren't getting promotions
- Always thinks they're under-appreciated.
- Has been there and done that, but it's surprisingly not provable.

There are two kinds of know-it-alls: those who do know it all, and those who think they do. If Joanne fell into the first category, their irritating nature and team-disruptive behavior would be offset by their knowledge and experience. Unfortunately, Joanne is in the second group, which just makes her disruptive.

Write Out a List of Employees You Have That Fit This Description

Before We Move On...

The ten employee types just described can be a small problem, or they can be quite difficult. You may choose to coach Andy, Barry, Cassie, Darrel, Ellen, Frank, Gabby, Harriet, Irvine, and Joanne to improve their behavior. You might find ways to make them work within the team. You might not. But there's one type of employee that you shouldn't waste the time and resources on, and you'll always regret it if you try.

#11
The "Toxic" Employee

This person displays any three of the behaviors of the ten types already described. They're like poison running through the veins of your team. You simply cannot keep this employee, and any attempt to do so will damage the rest of your team in a severe way.

To build the right team, you must start with an accepting canvas. The Toxic Employee is not accepting of anything or anyone. How many of your excellent team members have been punished because they had to do the work of the Toxic Employee – because you didn't do anything about them?

Many books spend a hundred pages on what you can do with difficult employees, and the truth is, you shouldn't give up easily on worthwhile people. The Toxic Employee is not worthwhile – not to your team anyway. The courageous thing, the kind thing, the right thing to do is to simply ditch the Toxic Employee. It didn't take a hundred pages – we saved a lot of trees today.

Write Out a List of Employees You Have That Fit This Description

#12
The "Employee of The Month"

Looking for that stable employee... the one you want to clone. This is the person who should serve as the model of an attitude, behaviors, and personality when you're looking to fill the gaps in your team.

This may not be the smartest person (though it often is), nor are they the most creative or the best decision-maker. They might have a few quirks in their personality, such as unbending paper clips and leaving them on everyone's desk, like a trail of breadcrumbs in case they get lost. Maybe they hum a Village People tune for three hours out of every day. So what?

This is an employee who works as a team member, picks up the slack for others, asks for help when it's needed, doesn't mind being told they're wrong and is willing to express a risky opinion. This is the person you want on your team.

This employee is, you might guess already, the opposite of the other eleven.

The Keys to Being the Employee of the Month (or Year, Decade, etc.)

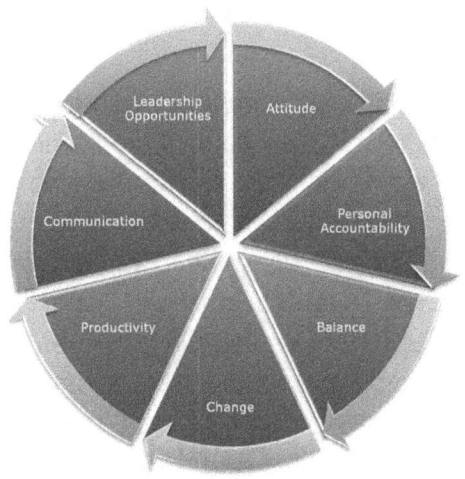

What is it about them?

- **They're accountable.** They accept credit for those things they do right, and responsibility for errors they make. They'll never say "It wasn't my fault."

  Unlike the Complainer Betty or "It's Not My Job" Frank, The Employee of The Month accepts the fate of the team together; They work toward helping others, not protecting themselves.

- **They understand balance.** The Employee of the Month might not be there 60 hours a week all the time – they have a life - but you know if you did need it they would be willing.

  Your Employee of The Month enjoys their work, but will also have interests and passions outside of work. This is critical! If work is all they have, then they're out of balance.

  When you find your best employees, you'll discover that they each have something besides work that makes them excited, something that they love to do. It might be sailing, it might be collecting stamps, or it might be grandchildren – but it is something that makes life better outside the office, which makes life better inside the office.

They understand that success is not permanent – but neither is failure. They celebrate victories but doesn't forget that there's more to do. They get disappointed, but only as long as is necessary before looking for the next challenge.

- **They embrace change**. While the Anti-Change Agent will find something wrong with every new thing, this person will look for what is right. How we "used to do it" only has value if it worked, and there are always ways to improve.

- **They're Productive**. Productivity is never an accident. It is always the result of a commitment to excellence, intelligent planning, and focused effort.

- **They communicate with passion and courage**. Someone with great ideas must be willing to voice them. Someone must be willing to look at the Emperor's New Clothes and say "I can't see it."

- **They seek leadership opportunities**. The Employee of The Month doesn't think they should have your job. They aren't there to usurp but to support, by stepping into any leadership opportunities when they present themselves. As Harriet Ford said, "Whether you think you can or can't, either way, you're right."

This person understands their skills, and the limitation of those skills. They're willing to take a chance, but only when the risk is reasonable, and the reward is worthwhile to the team.

- They're a full-fledged member of the cult, with **ATTITUDE**.

As we've said before, no one is perfect. Just as someone might exhibit one or more characteristics of those "bad" employees, someone might show one or more of those good Employees of The Month characteristics. It's not a checklist for passing or failing scores – it's a guideline of things to look for in your people that tell you they're on the right track.

Of what long-term value is this list of twelve employees when building your team? Hopefully, the value is obvious. Once you've identified those who are damaging to your team, you can be that courageous leader who sits down and tells them about The Question, and describes why you feel how you do. Then, if this is possible, you can find ways to help that person be a more productive member of your team... or make that hard yet necessary decision to remove them from your team.

Write Out a List of Employees You Have That Fit This Description

NOTE

NOTE

THE DECISION
TO FIRE

The Economics of Firing

"You're Fired."

We've talked a lot about people who don't belong in your team, and whether they should be removed. When it's necessary, of course, it's necessary – but it's not a decision that you should enter lightly or without a clear confidence that it **truly IS necessary**.

Several well-regarded studies have recently estimated the cost of losing an employee. I think this is an extremely conservative number. The Society for Human Resource Management (SHRM) estimated that it costs $3,500 to replace one $8/hour employee when all costs – recruiting, interviewing, hiring, training, reduced productivity, etc. - are factored in.

Other sources provide these estimates: It costs you 30-50% of the annual salary for entry-level employees, 150% of middle-level employees, and up to 400% for high-level or specialized employees.

Think of a job in your organization where there has been some turnover, perhaps supervisors. Estimate their annual average pay and the number of supervisors you lose each year. For example, if their annual salary is $40,000, multiply this by 1.25 (125% of their annual pay, a conservative estimate). This means it costs $50,000 to replace one supervisor.

So, if this company loses ten supervisors a year, then it takes $500,000 in replacement costs. That's the bottom line cost – what's the top line cost? If a company's profit margin is 10%, then it takes $5,000,000 in revenues to replace those ten supervisors.

So, no – it should not be entered into carelessly or without due consideration. This is serious business – but there will be times when the cost of keeping someone obviously outweighs the cost of replacing them.

> If you need to fire someone, and you feel good about it, that's bad.

> If you need to fire someone and you feel guilty about it, that's worse.

You should fire someone when they have the tools and the training to do that job, but can't or won't do it. If they can't, you're doing them a favor my starting them on the new path toward a better life. If they won't, you're protecting your team – AND you're helping them on a path toward a better life. In either case, you'll do it because it needs to be done for all people. You should be able to do this without regret or hesitation. If you cannot accept that this is a part of building a team... well, then you should be the one moving on.

PERFORMANCE
EVALUATIONS

THE KEY TO TEAM MAINTENANCE AND GROWTH

Annual reviews are not enough. Semi-annual reviews are not enough. Performance reviews are, in reality, a daily occurrence. Every day, for every task, people should know what they did well, what they didn't do well, and what you expect out of them tomorrow. These are not formal, written reviews, but feedback they will come to expect, and the use of which will ward off problems and surprises when the formal performance reviews arrive.

Performance Evaluation Basics

If there's a measuring stick as to whether your performance review process is successful, it's this: **Nothing in the formal performance review should ever be a surprise**. If you're bringing up any performance issue – good or bad – for the first time during the formal process, you haven't done your job. You haven't been giving daily accurate feedback. The formal performance evaluation should be a moment of confirmation, agreement, and plan of action.

Evaluating an employee's performance is a critical task for a manager or owner of a company. Determining how you will evaluate each of your employees is the tough part. Each person should know what is expected of them and what their goals are for the upcoming evaluation period. Below are six tips that will help to make your next evaluation conference be a success:

- **Make It Specific** - When evaluating an employee, make sure that you are evaluating them on criteria that can be evaluated based on accomplishments. Avoid goals based on criteria that can be interpreted several different ways. "Doing a good job" might sound positive, but it's vague. How did they do a good job? Why was it good? What made it good?

- **Measurement** - When evaluating your employee's performance, make sure that there are ways to measure it. Set specific goals and points in time for them to be measured to see if the employee has completed the tasks assigned and met the goals.

- **Challenge the Employee** - Challenge your employee with the goals that you have set for them, but make sure they are not so demanding that they are impossible to achieve. Goals should encourage an employee, stretch their skills to develop them, but not make them feel overwhelmed.

- **Tie in the Company Goals** - The goals that you set for your employee and evaluate them on should be accomplishments that help the company meet its own goals as well. Do not set goals that have no bearing on the company's success. Remember, you serve the greater whole as well as your team.

- **Time Frame** - Set a time for you and each of your employees to meet and evaluate if they have met their goals. When evaluating an employee, you should have a time frame in mind for them to complete each of their goals. Agreement on those goals is essential – the employee must believe, as you do, that they can be met.

- **All Employees Are Not Equal** - Know the skills of your employees. Not every employee will be a top performer. Set goals based on the skill set that each employee brings to the job. Some are Superman, but many of us are simply Clark Kent.

Performance Appraisal Methods

Performance appraisals are conducted by companies in order to evaluate the strengths and weaknesses of the employees; the frequency and methods of the performance appraisals are determined by the company. There are several performance appraisal methods that can be used to provide feedback on employee performance.

The purpose of performance appraisals is to provide feedback on an employee's performance, provide the basis for a merit increase, create a development plan, and provide the foundation for future promotions.

- **Management by Objectives (MBO)** - The Management by Objectives (MBO) performance appraisal method depends on the employee and manager agreeing to certain objectives, followed by the employee submitting status reports periodically. The employee's final rating is based upon their performance compared with the objectives.

- **Ranking** - The ranking method compares one employee against another, with a range going from best to worst; the standard bell curve is the distribution that results. Most employees will be in the middle, while the very best and the very worst are at the ends.

- **Rating Scale** - The rating scale method of performance appraisal involves simply grading an employee's performance. The check boxes may be "yes/no" or range from satisfactory to unsatisfactory.

- **Narrative** - The narrative method can be used in conjunction with the other methods and allows the employee and the manager to write statements about the employee's performance.

Appraisals and Merit Raises

Performance appraisals are a management-evaluation process that provides feedback on employee performance. This evaluation and documentation of employee perform- ance provides a basis for merit raises and promotions. Whe- ther or not the timing of the merit adjustments to pay corre- late with the timing of the performance appraisal process and meeting is really not the important issue - the issue is the correlation between these two important events. Here are a few important issues to keep in mind with regards to the success of an appraisal program:

- **Significance** - Performance appraisals in- clude written and oral feedback that should provide employees with specific steps to im- prove their performance.

- **Function** - Performance appraisals can also serve the purpose of clarifying job re- sponsibilities, improving communication between superiors and subordinates, and providing evidence of an organization's commitment to developing employees.

- **Benefits** - Linking merit raises with performance appraisals give the evaluation process immediate validity and significance, while also increasing the reliability and objectivity of managerial decisions on promotions and pay adjustments.

- **Considerations** - Performance appraisals are often resented by employees because they are commonly used to objectively build a case to terminate an employee; linking raises and promotions with employee appraisals decreases this resentment. Remember: Nothing in a performance appraisal should ever come as a surprise!

- **Warnings** - Any source or evidence of "rater bias" in employee appraisals will counteract all the goals and benefits of performance appraisals and can result in employee backlash, especially when the process is tied to merit raises.

Take A Look Inside

Truly, truly, truly, promote from within your organization whenever possible. If you are not producing leaders, you're not producing results within your company. There are times, of course, when that is not possible; when the skill set and the experience needed simply cannot be found within, you serve the team – and the greater whole – by looking outside the organization for the right person.

If you use all the due diligence and tools talked about in this book so far, you'll find the right person. When the right person – or even approximately the right person – already works for your team (or the company as a whole), you send the right message of success, accomplishment, and loyalty, by promoting that internal candidate.

NOTES

NOTES

THE PROCESS OF
TEAM (RE)BUILDING

TEAM REBUILDING

We're coming toward the end of the journey. You've either read this book in one sitting – maybe on a plane to pass the time or at the end of the night when there's really nothing good on television – or you've taken it in small segments. Regardless, it's time to summarize the process so you can more easily put these tools to work for you immediately. The following is a standard process model that works in various areas of business. It is referred to as the **PDA Process Model: Plan – Do – ACT.**

Plan

- Make a void in your team.
- Evaluate "strength points" and "weakness points" within your existing team.
- Decide what you need and want to fill that void.
- Create a strategic action plan

The void in your team may have been a Toxic Employee or just an expansion of your current team needs. Before you go looking, make sure you know exactly what you're looking for – this might be a discussion with the team about their needs.

Have a clear vision of the skills, experience, and most of all attitude you want in a new team member. Write it down, refer to it, and make it a part of you. Finally, create a written plan for your next steps. Remember, you're finding a partner for you, your team, and the company as a whole, so this will always be serious business.

Do

- Source applicants.
- Evaluate resumes.
- Perform phone interviews
- Take time to prepare for in-person inter-views.
- Develop an interview guide
- Perform behavior-based interviews and use the 80/20 Rule.
- Complete profiles and assessments
- Perform a second interview (maybe a group interview).
- Check references.
- Extend an educated contingent offer.
- Close the deal.

It's an unfortunate fact of business that the need to hire someone can arrive suddenly, through sickness or death, family emergencies, unexpected employee decisions, and many other reasons.

The void may arrive quickly, but to transfer that urgency to the hiring process, and thereby skipping the many critical steps, is a mistake that will cost many more times what it would otherwise cost to replace a productive employee – because you'll end up often doing it again and again. Taking a page from the carpenter's creed – measure twice and cut once – we should hire slowly to keep them a long time.

Act

- Roll out the red carpet and make the introduction to your company stellar.
- Be prepared to spend plenty of time with your team member on their first day.
- Have their workspace clean, business cards ready, and uniforms available if appropriate.
- Don't shortchange them by expecting them to learn everything on the fly.
- Make sure you formally introduce them to the rest of the team – don't let it happen accidentally.

Many years ago, my first day on the job as maintenance manager happened the same way it probably happened to most of you at one point. I arrived fresh and ready to the maintenance office at 9:00 am. About fifteen minutes later my boss happened in. He tossed a bunch of papers at me and told me that I should fill those out during lunch and be sure to have them back to him by the end of the day.

He then went over to a locker and pulled out an old, dirty uniform with "DOUG" emblazoned on the front. "If things work out," he said, "you'll get new uniforms in a couple weeks." He tossed me a set of keys, walked out the door and said, "If you need anything, find me. But don't need me too often."

Does that sound at all familiar? Many of us in this situation will figure things out; we adapt, and we make the best of the situation. But does this kind of approach inspire us at all? It's safe to say that we want better for our team. We hired this person because in our estimation they were special – let's treat them how we envision them; let's show them we deserve that specialness.

Staying Objective

We Don't have To Agree...
We Just Have To Agree That We Don't Have To
Agree

This book talks about identifying people who aren't right for your team – but at no time should you ever expect your team to be a perfect mesh of personalities and ideas. Remember, it's the differences between us that makes life interesting. If we hire people just like us, all we do is make our strength redundant and our weaknesses stronger.

Embrace difference, and always work on keeping your decisions based on what is best for the team, not an emotional reaction to something irrelevant.

Three common areas where people differ are Beliefs, Communication Styles, and Thinking Styles.

Beliefs

By beliefs, we're not talking about whether or not you believe in God, aliens, or the right to wear silly hats... we're talking about everyday mundane beliefs that can cause conflict, such as what is the right thing to say, what is the right thing to do. The problem is, we have two "rights" in our world – *real* right and *perceived* right.

Most people would agree on many of the *real* rights – for example: it's not right to kill or to steal, but it's right to be compassionate to other people.

Even then there are gray areas and uncertainties. We have "justifiable" homicide in the case of self-defense or defense of others; compassion, some people say, must be earned, not freely given; and so on. But disagreements on these are less frequent, and typically these don't create workplace or daily conflicts.

What about *perceived* right?

When you were growing up, you may have been told, "Don't put your elbows on the table!" I recall that happened to me or one of my brothers and sisters at least once a night. Didn't you ask, or want to ask, "Why?" What is it about putting your elbows on the table that is so horribly bad? Are we concerned that we'll upset the balance of the table legs and bring the whole thing crashing to the floor? Does anyone else (other than parents) feel insulted when they see elbows on the table? Are my elbows somehow offensive to you?

Zig Ziglar told a story about a young mother teaching her 10-year-old daughter to cook. She was careful to explain every step of the process to the girl, including the reasons why things were done how they were done – understanding the reasons, she knew, made for better learning.

As the mother brought out the ham and got ready to put it in the pan she said, "then before you place the ham in the pan, you cut a little off each end, like this." She demonstrated cutting about a 1" slice off of each end. The little girl, naturally, asked, "Why do you do that?" The mother thought for a moment, and said, "It's just how it's always done – my mother taught me to do it that way, and her mother taught her before that – it makes the ham better."

The young girl wasn't satisfied with the answer, so when they next visited her grandma she asked her, "Granny, why do you cut the ends off of a ham before you put it in the oven?" Granny, happy to hear that her granddaughter was taking an interest in domestic arts, said, "Well, honey, that's the way you have to do it. My mother taught me that when I was very young."

Still not fully satisfied, the young girl called great-grandma, now living in a retirement home in Arizona, and asked the 85-year-old shuffleboard player, "Great-grandma, why do we cut the ends off the ham before we put it in the oven?" Great-grandma said, "Well, my dear, when I was a young housewife we had to do that – we only had one roasting pan, and it was too small. We had to cut the ends off to fit it in the pan."

What is right can be different things to different people. That's where a lot of your difficulties will come from, and they can be the major stumbling block. You can't change another person's beliefs and values – certainly not in a short period of time and not when we deal with most people on the level we do, in a limited way and for specific purposes. When you deal with someone whose value system differs from yours, it can frustrate you – after all, we all think we're right. And sometimes – we all are right.

Communication Styles

Some people are very open, sharing their opinions and perceptions freely. Others are more self-contained – that is, they tend to keep things to themselves, talking about their opinions and perceptions very little, if at all. In some instances, this mixture works well – in some relationships, whether personal or professional, having one person who takes the active role and one who takes the passive role in communications can offer a good balance. There's no right or wrong in this, just different styles.

However, when the efficient exchange of ideas is necessary, there can be difficulties. For example, if you're a self-contained person, preferring to speak only when you have something worthwhile to say, dealing with someone who spouts off every thought and idea that comes into their head, whether it's worthwhile or not, can be irritating. I mean, why can't they think a little before they speak, right?

On the other hand, for someone who is expressive of ideas and thoughts, someone who thinks that it's better to get something out there where people can evaluate it, dealing with someone who keeps everything to themselves and who refuses to have an opinion, can be just as irritating. After all, have some guts and speak your mind, right?

Both of these people can be frustrated, not because the other person is wrong, but merely because they have differing styles and aren't quite sure how to bridge the gap between them.

Some people are very direct – they are decisive and will confront you if there is conflict. Compare this to an indirect person; whom may make slower decision, will analyze the facts thirty times before doing anything, and tried to avoid conflict wherever possible.

When these communication styles interact, there is naturally some difficulty. What do direct people often think about those indirect people? They sometimes consider them weak, wimpy, indecisive. Those who are less direct have the opposing few of those direct people: they are overbearing, pushy, and reckless.

But are most people really that way? The styles are true, but the labels aren't. Successful people, both in personal and business ventures, come from all walks of life, and encompass all the styles and differences. In different situations we exhibit different tendencies. We aren't all one or all another, and it changes with the situation. Even those extreme people, those who are very direct or extremely indirect, are successful – which means it can't be wrong, it's just different.

These are styles, not states of being. They are habits and tendencies, and the labels we put on them are based on our own perceptions. These are important points to remember as we move forward.

Thinking Styles

When faced with important choices or a huge decision, do you consider yourself and objective person, or a subjective person?

What does the objective person do? They might take a piece of paper, make a column for the PROS and a column for the CONS of the decision, and list them carefully. They might give different weight to the factors based on their importance, and then they'll weigh the alternatives and choose the one which seems, objectively, to offer the best chance of success, based on his objective evaluation.

The subjective person ignores PROS and CONS and does what they want – or what their "gut feeling" tells them is the right thing. Perhaps they'll make a chart, list the PROS and CONS, give weight to things as they feel their importance merits, decides which is the best alternative.... THEN does what they wanted to or their gut feeling tells them to anyway!

Don't discount the value of an emotional response. In his book Emotional Intelligence, Daniel Goleman presents evidence that what we call gut feeling or intuition, is often based on past experiences, on information that we're not consciously aware of, but our subconscious mind knows well. When we see the right choice (or wrong choice) and feel sure about it - even if we don't know why - it could be that part of our mind which knows more than we do, cluing us in.

What about those who decide to flip a coin? What thinking style are they practicing? If they've decided that both options (we're assuming two possibilities, for the sake of simplicity) are of equal value – or of equal danger – then they leave it to chance.

Is this objective?

You could argue that it is – after all, each choice has the same value and risk. Is this being subjective but unwilling to decide? You could argue that as well since with both options seemingly equal, and there's no added danger or benefit in either; so, flipping a coin is just an unnecessary extra step.

In actually, there are few true coin-flippers. An objective person isn't going to flip a coin. If both choices seem equal on the surface, they'll dig a little deeper and find a difference in the details that they can quantify – assign value – and make a choice based on those details. If time doesn't allow for more analysis, then they'll simply pick one, knowing that the coin isn't going to have any better shot that they would at making the so-call right choice.

A subjective person will flip the coin, but in that split second when the result is revealed, they'll have an emotional reaction – either relief or sadness. This will lead them to what they really wanted to choose – again, that gut feeling.

We have to embrace the differences because that's a huge part of what makes a team work. We live in a world where a pro football player can revive his career and image by being a contestant on a prime-time network TV dancing show. Anything is possible!

NOTES

NOTES

NOW WHAT?

NOW WHAT?

Hopefully, you've armed yourself with the answer to that question already:

- You've picked up tools for evaluating your existing team.
- You've identified the Toxic Employees.
- You've asked "The Question" about your team members and made decisions about how to act on the answer.
- You've reviewed your hiring processes and reinforced the need for complete and special attention to finding your next team member.
- Maybe you've even found a bit more...

It's extremely difficult to write about business in general terms because they all have one thing in common – they are all different.

You will always know more about your business than I will. As mentioned early in the book, you will find some tools worthwhile and rush out to use them, and you might find that others don't apply to your business, or you don't agree with them, and simply ignore them.

Here is my personal guarantee to you...

Embrace and engage a careful process, and it will reap huge rewards!

If I could choose the five things that I hope you'll choose to accept, embrace, and act upon, it would be these Five *"Hire The Best – Ditch The Rest"* precepts:

1. Make hiring a process, which has specific steps you consistently follow without fail. Use every resource that is available.

2. Have a clear picture of exactly who you want before you start the process. This doesn't mean you'll know their age, gender, appearance, hobbies, or favorite TV program, but it does mean you'll know the specific set of skills and the personality type that will fit with your team.

3. Take your time. Urgency, again, is that silver bullet that will kill your success. If you spend more time hiring, you'll spend less time firing.

4. When you consider candidates, look for that person who is willing and ready to join your cult. If you have the choice between a well-trained and experienced normal person, and a trainable cult-follower, give real consideration to the nutcase.

5. Look at your potential bad employees. Ask The Question regularly. The Toxic employee is not just bad for themselves; they're a cancer that can grow and spread to other parts of your organization. Even after they're gone, they can still infect your team, if you failed to take decisive and timely action to remove them from the company.

In business, there are no magic elixirs, or even a potion to solve all your troubles and soothe your pains. You can, however, find plenty of poisons, which requires time to heal from, or take some preventive care and follow these five "Hire the Best – Ditch the Rest" precepts, and spend the remaining of your time being successful rather than trying to put out fires.

NOTES

NOTES

APPENDIXES
QUICK-REFERENCE VERSIONS
OF THE IMPORTANT POINTS

APPENDIX A

TEN KEYS TO A HAPPY WORKPLACE

An excerpt from the upcoming book
Appropriate Irreverence: Building a Company
Culture That Will Thrive in This Generation
-Richard S. George.

Throughout my career, I have asked bosses what fulfils employees at work, and the answers are traditionally things or tangible rewards such as: a good salary, a pleasant office, generous benefits, etc. These play a role, of course, but increasingly my research shows that real satisfaction depends heavily on intangibles like respect, trust, and fairness.

Real workplace happiness has two components: the individual and the company.

Sally Haver, senior vice president of the Ayers Group, says, "You can be generally speaking happy in your work but not happy in your company, due to a bad boss, a bad corporate culture, or a colleague who makes your life miserable." These are all things that become incumbent on you the boss to fix. This is the reason that people say people don't typically leave companies; they leave bosses.

These Suggestions Are Written as an Open Letter to People In Management or Supervisory Roles Everywhere.

For me to feel committed to your organization, your team, and your crew, I need to have basic needs fulfilled. Leaders spend their lives telling team members what that Leader wants and expects, so here is a list of things that we want from you as our Leader:

1. **Don't micromanage me:** tell me my role, tell me what to do, and give me the rules. I require clear direction and parameters, so I can work within the clearly defined and broad boundaries. Most of all, don't expect me to guess what my job is or what you want my performance to be.

2. **Discipline us:** especially my coworker who is out of line. I often think, "I wish my supervisor would tell [coworker] that their behavior is unacceptable." People need to be held accountable for their action, but in a fair and just way, so others can learn from those mistakes to also know what is and isn't acceptable.

3. **Appreciate me:** Stop treating praise like it is an expensive thing. Stop going out of your way to tell what I do wrong and start making an effort to find what I do right. Motivate me by leveraging my strengths, not harping on my weaknesses.

4. **Don't scare me:** Don't lose your temper at meetings because we didn't meet your expectations. This doesn't motivate me; in fact, it does quite the opposite. Also, I really don't need to know about everything that worries you. I respect that you trust me, but you are the boss.

5. **Impress me:** Strong leaders impress me in a variety of ways. Yes, some are great examples of management, but others are simply bold and courageous, and still others are creative and smart. Strong leaders bring strength to an organization by providing a characteristic that others don't have.

6. **Trust & autonomy:** Give me something interesting to work on and trust me with that opportunity. I am a person that will always make decisions with you and the company in mind because I want to be part of a winning team.

7. **Help us win:** Nobody wants to fail; yet, putting people in the wrong roles, setting unrealistic goals, and not firing problematic employees, sets a precedent that you want us to fail. This leaves us frustrated and makes us feel defeated. If that is not what you want, then look at what you're doing.

8. **Give me a voice:** You hired me because I had something that you liked. Why is it that after the interview, my opinion became a thing of the past? I am a grown-up and I can accept the fact that you might disagree with my opinion; I will not run crying into the night if my idea is not adopted.

9. **Get me excited:** I need a purpose for what I do, what the company does, and what the product does. Tell me why it is necessary. Get me excited. Give me a sense of purpose for continuing with a stellar performance. It is easy for me to become acceptable of the status quo if you readily accept it too.

10. **Winning team:** A team that wins has no fear of losing jobs. I want to feel stable and secure in my position. I want to know that there are growth opportunities for me somewhere in the future. When I feel that we are part of the losing team, I feel that sense of security and stability slipping away, and this causes me stress.

Most employees find happiness at work when they feel connected to the organization. Understanding that career contentment is different from job satisfaction is the primary key to success. Job satisfaction comes and goes but finding contentment in your career is a lifelong mindset and becomes a quest for many employees. If you build their Utopia they will move in and not keep their packing boxes.

I have stayed at jobs that did not have the best pay or benefits because of the culture, and I have left jobs that had great pay and benefits because of the culture. I guarantee you that if you invest in some of these intangibles, it will save you money and make each and every day of your life better.

APPENDIX B
The Five *"Hire the Best –*
Ditch the Rest" Precepts

1. Make hiring a process, which has specific steps you consistently follow without fail. Use every resource that is available.

2. Have a clear picture of exactly who you want before you start the process. This doesn't mean you'll know their age, gender, appearance, hobbies, or favorite TV program, but it does mean you'll know the specific set of skills and the personality type that will fit with your team.

3. Take your time. Urgency, again, is that silver bullet that will kill your success. If you spend more time hiring, you'll spend less time firing.

4. When you consider candidates, look for that person who is willing and ready to join your cult. If you have the choice between a well-trained and experienced normal person, and a trainable cult-follower, give real consideration to the nutcase.

5. Look at your potential bad employees. Ask The Question regularly. The Toxic employee is not just bad for themselves; they're a cancer that can grow and spread to other parts of your organization. Even after they're gone, they can still infect your team, if you failed to take decisive and timely action to remove them from the company.

APPENDIX C

Rules For Asking The Question....

- **The Question** should never be asked when you're mad at your employee. It's not something to be tainted by emotions. It's a regular, but not daily, evaluation of that person's overall value to the team.

- **The Question** should be based on skills, attitude, and affect on the rest of the team, not your opinion of their style or personal beliefs. It's not an excuse for getting rid of someone you don't agree with.

- Each answer to **The Question** demands some type of action. If you would be devastated, take steps to make sure it doesn't happen. If you would be indifferent, find out why and work to make that person able to devastate you. If you would be relieved, you must choose either to fire or fix the issues.

- DON'T KEEP IT A SECRET!

APPENDIX D

Seven Steps to Having That Courageous Conversation

1. Choose the person that you don't feel 100% about.
2. Identify clearly the truth/core of what you want to express.
3. Identify the worst possible outcome you can imagine.
4. Accept that possibility. Now, let it go.
5. Remember that it's OK to feel uncomfortable, even terrified. In fact, you probably should feel uncomfortable; that will add the compassion piece to your message. The greater the fear, the more you have to gain.
6. Embrace the moment; this is the equivalent to crowning the first giant hill of a rollercoaster. You are now committed to a prosperous future.
7. Go For It! Accept what you get as the best possible outcome.

APPENDIX E

The Four Hiring Truths

What They Know Changes, Who They Are Doesn't

You Can't Find What You're Not Looking For

The Best Way to Evaluate People Is To Watch Them Work

You Can't Hire People Who Don't Apply

APPENDIX G
The Twelve Employees
(And how to spot them)

The "Not So Go Getter"	The "Complainer"
The "Paycheck Gatherer"	The "Anti-Change Agent"
The "Overwhelmed Employee"	The "That's Not My Job" Employee
The "Socialite" Employee	The "Clockwatcher"
The "Nosey" Employee	The "I Deserve Your Job" Employee
The "Toxic" Employee	The "Employee of the Month"

#1
The "Not-So Go-Getter"

- Just moves along through the day
- Does what they're told – no more and no less
- Has no natural initiative instincts

#2
The "Complainer"

- Whines about everything
- Complains whether it is bad or good
- Tells others that all good things have ulterior motives

#3
The "Paycheck Gatherer"

- Always concerned about payroll: When is it coming? Will it be late? How about a raise?
- When they spend money, it's your responsibility to cover the cost.
- Many conversations center around what they're "entitled" to".

#4
The "Anti-Change Agent"

- Fights every change in the team or the organization, no matter how slight.
- Policies, procedures, job descriptions, and even the color of the walls were all better "the way we used to do it."

#5
The "Overwhelmed" Employee

- Can never find enough time in the day to create more chaos.
- Spends more time worrying and talking about what they have to do than actually doing what they have to do.

#6
The "That's Not My Job" Employee

- Their job description should be taken literally, but only using their own literal definition.
- They think life should be fair and everything should run as they expects it to run.
- Has no understanding of the team concept.

#7
The "Socialite" Employee

- Distracts the attention of others by constantly talking.
- Often the source of the latest rumors.
- Facts are not important; those can be made up along the way.

#8
The "Clockwatcher"

- Will always know exactly how many minutes (maybe seconds) they have to wait before 5:00 pm.
- Is much like the Paycheck Gatherer in that his main concern is their pay, not their accomplishments or the team.

#9
The "Nosey" Employee

- Always seems to know all the dirt.
- Mysteriously knows what everyone makes in salary.
- Seems to know where you are (or should be) at all times.
- Never seems to know they're failing.

#10
The "I Deserve Your Job" Employee

- Was hired into an entry level position and cannot understand why you didn't just step down and let them take over.
- Always thinks they're under-appreciated.
- Has been there and done that, but it's surprisingly not provable.

#11
The "Toxic" Employee

- Hard to miss! This person displays any three other behaviors already described. They're like poison running through the veins of your team. You simply cannot keep this employee, and any attempt to do so will damage the rest of your team in a severe way.

#12
The "Employee of the Month"

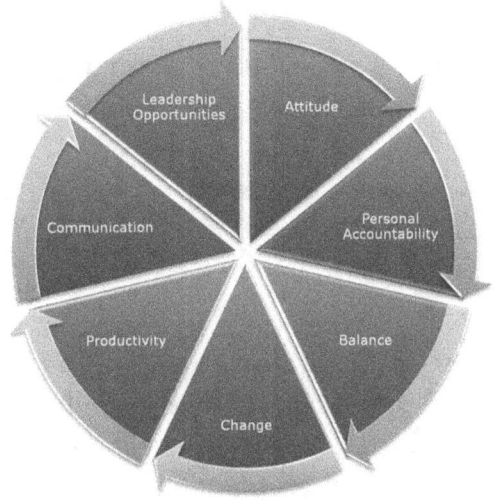

- They're accountable.
- They understand balance.
- They embrace change.
- They're productive.
- They communicate with passion and courage.
- They seek leadership opportunities.
- They're a full-fledged member of the cult, with ATTITUDE.

APPENDIX G

Q. How can I motivate the people in my department?
A. You can't.
(Reprinted from Stop Time Theft by Richard Buchko. Used with permission.)

It's the most popular question asked of trainers, motivational speakers, and authors. We all want our people to be motivated to work harder, to be more productive, and to accomplish greater things. How, we ask, can we do that?

You cannot motivate someone; not directly. All you can do is provide the right circumstances, environment, and tools for them to motivate themselves.

But wait, you say, if I tell someone that the report has to be on my desk by 10:15 AM the next day or they will be fired, and the report is done on time, didn't I motivate that person? If I give someone a raise, aren't I motivating them?

To answer that we have to clarify the difference between motivation and movement. If I walk into the room and see the cat lying on the floor in my path, and to get the cat out of my way I kick him clear across the room, what happened? The cat certainly moved, but was he motivated to do it? Did he want to? No, the cat moved, but I was motivated!

Movement is not motivation. Motivation is the long-term desire to achieve better results, and is based on each person's individual needs and desires. It not enough to set up rewards and punishments, because only a very small number of people will be motivated long-term by these practices.

154

Some of the motivators that have more lasting effect than rewards and punishment are job security, feeling of belonging or teamwork, and competition. You can help to create the environment where a person can finds these factors, but you don't motivate them, because you probably will never know what it is that works for that person - he or she might not even know.

What about money? Isn't money a motivator? Money is always good, but most often when we offer money it's a reward for something already accomplished, not for future good work. It might spur us on, just as the kicking the cat spurs the cat across the room, and threats of being fired might spur me on to action – for a while. If someone hates his job, money won't motivate him on to do much more than the minimum.

Fear? Constant threats of being fired will soon bring about the realization (real or imagined) that eventually he will be fired, and that certainly cannot spur him on to action beyond the minimum.

Do you want more than the bare minimum? Provide an environment where people can find their own motivators and reach them. Steer away from punishments and rewards (except where needed or appropriate), and concentrate on creating a stronger team, an atmosphere of security, daily challenges, and appreciation for what your people do. These are motivators!

NOI COACH™

NOI - NET OPERATING INCOME

Net Operating Income (NOI) is the single best indicator of overall performance. NOI Coach is a business consulting and coaching firm focusing on what is important to every company: growth of the bottom line. Here at NOI Coach we believe in the adage that "companies are perfectly designed to get the results they are getting" and the transformation of any company is solely based on a re design of their model.

NOI Coach develops your blueprint for success while guiding you through our coaching, consulting and educational programs. A Strategic Action Plan designed to give you substantial results will serve as your roadmap of the future. Our unique 360° Evaluation explores the culture, strategy, core process and structure systems of your organization to determine how they affect your current results.

TRAINING – CONSULTING – COACHING - SUPPORT

If your vision is clear, then all your decisions should be informed by that vision. For example, decisions about who to hire, where to allocate funds and other resources, and issues of communication should be weighed against the outcomes you want vis-à-vis your vision. Some things may seem to be questionable in the short run, but perfect in the long term.

Strategic thinking is a way to examine your choices and being prepared, whether the outcome is positive or negative. Strategic thinking requires you to consider the elements, potential, and effects of your approaches, and to examine each with a critical, honest eye.

Think about what you really want, how to achieve it, who to include, and most important of all – what happens if you fail. Being prepared for a success is one thing, being prepared for a negative outcome is another.

NOI Coach can help clarify your vision and help you maintain balance between business strategies and personal strategies.

Your NOI Coach is Rich George, a successful business person that has over 20 years' experience. Rich brings a no-nonsense approach to strategic planning and a passion for culture building.

Rich's background includes the management of over two billion dollars of real estate assets, and over 50 million dollars of capital re-investment strategies. Key to his success is the management of highly distressed properties, including those in court receivership.

Rich attended Wayne State University and is a Licensed Real Estate Broker. He has been recognized by his peers as a leader in the industry serving on the Board of Directors for the Property Management Association of Michigan, and as the President of The Detroit Metropolitan Apartment Association. He was recognized as one of the first graduates of the Leadership Lyceum for the National Apartment Association and has served on a multitude of committees. Rich Is a current faculty member of the National Apartment Association Education Institute and the Military Lodging and Housing Institute.

Known for his team building, culture changing, and change management skills, Rich leads the market in promotion and preservation.

A Selection of Programs Available From NOI Coach

- Hire the Best - Ditch the Rest
- The 12 C's of Leadership – Leadership as seen in the movies
- Building High Performance Teams
- Developing High Performance Strategies
- NOI Strategies for the Next Generation
- Mastering Time Management
- Managing the "J" Curve of Change
- How to be the Employee that Successful Companies Fight to Keep
- L.E.A.R.N. Through Conflict – Dealing with Difficult People
- The Art of Successful Coaching
- How to Be Outstanding at Work and In Life
- Appropriate Irreverence – Building a Company Culture that Wins

And many others – call for more information!

NOI Coach is happy to create customized programs for its clients. Contact Rich at NOI coach to explore new oppor-tunities or to modify any of the above courses.

Let's see what we can do for you.

NOI Coach
A Division of Coach Services, Inc.
Waterford, MI
248-302-4444
visit www.noicoach.com

AVAILABLE NOW
The Twelve C's of an
Exceptional Leader

by Richard George

If you read this far, then I hope you've enjoyed Hire the Best – Ditch the Rest and plan to put these tools to work for you. Having the right team is essential, but once you have them, then the question becomes: what do you need to do to keep them?

As a former property manager, the habits I learned and processes to which I became addicted have enabled me to thrive. I am addicted to reading, I am addicted to pursuing knowledge, and I am addicted to making difficult situations simple. Leadership can be difficult, and I continue to strive for its simplicity.

Throughout my years of leadership, I have diligently tried to isolate the characteristics of good leaders. Many business books and ideological philosophies gave great insight to my quest, yet the real test was practicality and simple implementation.

I created the Twelve C's list of the leadership characteristics to which I have become addicted. Each of these characteristics are derived and learned from my property management experiences and each is both practical and simple.

Find it on Amazon.